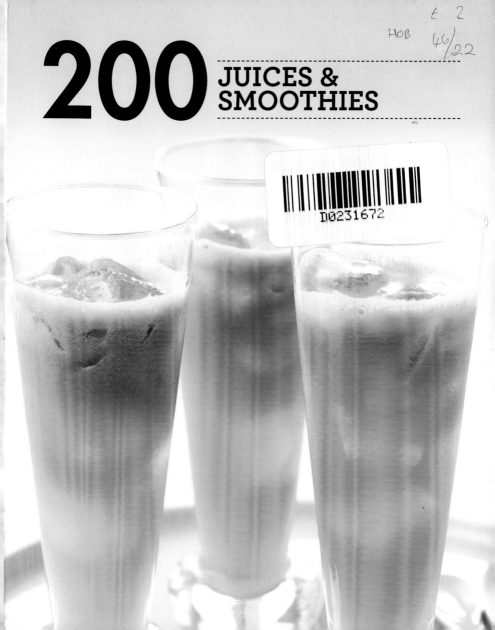

200

JUICES & SMOOTHIES

200

JUICES &
SMOOTHIES

An Hachette UK Company
www.hachette.co.uk

First published in Great Britain in 2008 by Hamlyn,
a division of Octopus Publishing Group Ltd,
Carmelite House, 50 Victoria Embankment,
London EC4Y 0DZ
www.octopusbooks.co.uk

This edition published in 2016

Copyright © Octopus Publishing Group Ltd 2008, 2016

The recipes in this book have previously appeared in other
books published by Hamlyn

ISBN 978-0-600-63330-3

A CIP catalogue record for this book is available from the
British Library

Printed and bound in China

10 9 8 7 6 5 4 3 2 1

Standard level spoon measurement are used in all recipes.
1 tablespoon = one 15 ml spoon
1 teaspoon = one 5 ml spoon

Both imperial and metric measures have been given in all
recipes. Use one set of measurements only and not a mixture
of both.

200 ml (7 fl oz) makes 1 average serving.

All fruit and vegetables should be washed before use.
Fresh herbs should be used unless otherwise stated.
All yogurt should be live unless otherwise stated.

This book includes dishes made with nuts and nut
derivatives. It is advisable for those with known allergic
reactions to nuts and nut derivatives and those who may be
potentially vulnerable to these allergies, such as pregnant and
nursing mothers, invalids, the elderly, babies and children, to
avoid dishes made with nuts and nut oils. It is also prudent to
check the labels of pre-prepared ingredients for the possible
inclusion of nut derivatives.

contents

introduction

juicing is the answer

These days it is impossible to escape the fact that we need to eat at least five portions of fruit and vegetables every day to make sure that we enjoy good health throughout our lives. Today's busy lifestyles mean that more often than not we find ourselves grabbing food as and when we can, giving little thought to its nutritional content and more to convenience and speed of preparation.

All research points to the fact, however, that both our long-term and short-term wellbeing depends on our being more careful about what we eat, especially when it comes

five good reasons to juice

● Juicing will help our bodies recover from illness and protect us against disease.

● Juicing can make sure that we get our daily recommended intake of vitamins and minerals easily.

● The folic acid found in fruit and vegetables contributes to both healthy hair and nails.

● The antioxidants in fruit and vegetables are essential for healthy, attractive skin.

● Juicing is a convenient and healthful way of supporting a weight-loss programme.

to fruit and vegetables. We should learn to regard food as an important and valuable commodity that will not only enable our bodies to perform at their optimum best for as long as possible but also improve our appearance.

nutritional benefits

Fruit and vegetables are cheap and easily available, and supermarkets and many smaller stores now offer a far wider range than ever before. Even though juicing requires practically no preparation and very little clearing up, many of us still find ourselves opting for a bag of crisps or a biscuit, rather than a fresh juice. Not only is there no nutritional value in junk food, but we will need to eat it more often and in greater quantities in order to feel satisfied.

It's perfectly understandable that most of us will find the idea of eating our way through a bag of apples or a pile of green vegetables every day hard work, and this is why juicing is such an attractive alternative: juices are quick and easy to prepare, they are delicious to drink, and they are satisfying and nourishing. Combining several different fruits and vegetables in your regular juices is one of the easiest ways of helping you achieve your quota of at least five a day in no time at all.

why juice at home?

So what is the difference between making your own juice and buying a carton? The most obvious difference is that the nutrients present in fresh, homemade juice far surpass anything you can buy. This is because bought juice has been pre-squeezed, packaged and usually diluted with water, so that many of the nutrients are lost along the way. There may also be additives in bought juices, including preservatives, whereas at home you can be sure of exactly what you are drinking.

Not only does homemade juice taste better, but the nutrients can be rapidly assimilated into the body. This can, in fact, be a bit of a shock to your body because it is a detoxification process that can cause a slight headache. When you begin to drink your own juices you might also find that you are passing water more often. However, once your body has adjusted to your new regime, the symptoms will fade and you will feel — and look — great.

making the best juices and smoothies

If you are a newcomer to juices and smoothies it is best not to rush out and buy a lot of expensive equipment. Smoothies can easily be made in a food processor or blender. However, if you are planning to make juices regularly you will find it is worth investing in a good machine.

which juicer?

There are several models of juicer on the market these days, and your choice will probably depend as much on how much you want to spend as to how effective the juicer will be. There are two basic options: a masticating juicer, which forces ingredients through a wire mesh, thereby extracting as much juice as possible as it does so, and a centrifugal juicer, which uses spinning blades to separate the pulp from the juice. The centrifugal juicer produces less juice, but it is a cheaper option for beginners.

let's juice

1 Assemble your ingredients, but don't prepare them until the last minute to avoid discoloration.

2 Wash or scrub ingredients that you are keeping whole — such as carrots or parsnips — and peel them only if absolutely necessary.

3 Roughly chop and weigh the ingredients according to the recipe.

what is a smoothie?

Unlike a juice, a smoothie is made in a food processor or blender. It is thicker than a juice, and most include extra ingredients such as yogurt, honey, ice cream or milk as well as fruit and juices. A smoothie is even quicker and easier to make than juice because all the ingredients go straight into the machine and are simply processed for a few seconds.

One of the best ways of making a really good smoothie is to use frozen fruits. The process of freezing means that the vitamins and nutrients are retained in the fruits, and frozen produce allows you to enjoy seasonal fruits and vegetables all year round. Your drink will be naturally chilled and won't need to be diluted with ice or chilled water.

juices & smoothies for kids

Making sure that your children get a minimum of five fruits and vegetables a day can be a battle, but juices and smoothies are a great way to make sure they get all the nutrients needed for a healthy, growing body. Most kids love them, and your life will be easier if you don't have to try and get them to eat broccoli.

choosing the best ingredients

There are very few fruit or vegetables that can't be used in juices and smoothies, and although the idea of eating portions of parsnips and pineapple together might not fill you with enthusiasm this combination works surprisingly well as a juice. However, there are a few firm favourites that appear time and time again, and following is a round-up of some of the best fruit and vegetables.

Buy organic fruit and vegetables whenever possible to avoid residual pesticides and wash or scrub them thoroughly before use to remove dirt and germs.

apples

Not only are apples full of antioxidants, but they have a naturally sweet flavour that complements sour and savoury ingredients really well. Use apples unpeeled or juice them whole, including the pips, to gain the maximum nutritional benefit — the antioxidant quercetin, for example, is found only in the skin. The fresher the apple the more vitamin C it will contain.

oranges and other citrus fruits

These are one of the best sources of vitamin C, and also one of the most popular mixers in juices and smoothies. Some recipes suggest that you remove the skin but leave some of the pith attached to the segments to increase the vitamin content of your drinks.

bananas

Bananas are especially useful in smoothies because they help to create a thick, smooth, tasty drink. Bananas can be peeled, sliced and frozen overnight to make a cool drink the next day. They are full of carbohydrates and an ideal energy booster or quick snack.

strawberries

Both beneficial and delicious, strawberries are a good source of vitamin C, calcium and potassium. To make the most of this universal favourite freeze the fruits when in season and add them to smoothies all year round.

pears

Pears are delicious in juices. Not only do they combine well with other fruits and vegetables, but they are also ideal for children because they rarely cause an allergic reaction. They are full of vitamin C, potassium and beta-carotene and a quick source of energy.

peaches

This fruit can be a boon if you suffer from stomach upsets because of its antioxidant qualities. It is also a good source of vitamin C.

apricots

Both fresh and dried apricots can be used in juices and smoothies. Dried apricots tend to be much sweeter than the fresh fruit but they have a high beta-carotene and potassium content.

cranberries

If you suffer from urinary infections cranberry juice could be the answer. The fruits are rich in vitamin C and potassium, and they are delicious in juices, adding a bittersweet flavour and vibrant colour.

blackberries

Rich in vitamin C and full of antioxidants, blackberries are good for building a healthy immune system. The fresh fruit freezes well and can be added to smoothies all year round.

mangoes

A mango will add an exotic flavour to drinks, and the fruit also contains a high level of vitamin C, fibre and potassium. It is a great fruit to keep on your shopping list.

watermelons

Yielding large amounts of juice, watermelons are a great antioxidant, detoxing and diuretic fruits. They are also a firm favourite with children because of their mild, sweet flavour.

avocados

Avocados are full of protein and are filling and nutritious. They are rich in vitamin E, which is beneficial to the skin and helps maintain healthy circulation. Eat avocados as soon as they are ripe as they start to lose important antioxidants as they ripen. Cut them and remove the skin and stones at the very last minute to avoid discoloration.

tomatoes

It is believed that tomatoes may help lower the risk of certain cancers, and this is attributed to the lycopene they contain. They are also high in vitamin C and fibre. Adding tomatoes to savoury juices boosts their nutrient content and makes them colourful.

carrots

Carrots are great energy food and are an aid to good digestion because of their fibre content; they are also full of beta-carotene and alpha-carotene, and are delicious in both fruit and vegetable juices.

spinach

Some people recoil at the idea of spinach in a drink, but, as the saying goes, don't knock it until you've tried it. Rich in iron and beta-carotene, spinach is great for vegetarians.

beetroot

Beetroot is a great source of folic acid and fibre. Surprisingly perhaps, it is delicious when combined with citrus fruits, making a tangy and colourful juice.

celery

Celery is a great cleanser and is rich in phyto-nutrients. A few sticks of celery produce a good yield of juice, and it is much more easily digested as juice than in its raw state.

ginger

Renowned in many traditional diets as an immunity booster, ginger helps to fight bugs with its high levels of zinc. It is also said to be settling for the stomach and is particularly useful for mothers-to-be who are suffering from morning sickness.

live yogurt

Live yogurt is a valuable source of calcium and vitamin D. It helps to maintain good health, because it contains cultures with health-giving properties. Including yogurt in a smoothie is a good way of giving a child who doesn't like milk a calcium boost.

soya

Soya is rich in protein and calcium. It makes an excellent alternative to dairy products for those who are lactose-intolerant, and it helps to lower cholesterol levels. It is also useful for controlling the symptoms of the menopause.

fruit juices

watermelon & strawberry juice

Makes **200 ml (7 fl oz)**

200 g (7 oz) **strawberries**,
  plus extra to serve (optional)
200 g (7 oz) **watermelon**
small handful of mint leaves,
  plus sprigs to decorate
2–3 **ice cubes**

Hull the strawberries. Skin and deseed the melon and cut the flesh into cubes.

Transfer the fruit to a food processor or blender, add the mint and process with a couple of ice cubes.

Pour into a glass, decorate with mint sprigs and whole or sliced strawberries, if liked, and serve immediately.

For watermelon & cranberry juice, simply replace the strawberries with the same quantity of cranberries and add 200 g (7 oz) cucumber. This makes a longer, more refreshing and slightly tangy drink.

watermelon & raspberry juice

Makes **350 ml (12 fl oz)**

about 300 g (10 oz)
  watermelon
125 g (4 oz) **raspberries**
2–3 **ice cubes**

Skin and deseed the melon and cut the flesh into cubes.
Juice the melon with the raspberries.

Pour into a glass, add a couple of ice cubes and
serve immediately.

For watermelon & orange juice, juice 2 oranges instead
of the raspberries.

papaya, raspberry & grapefruit juice

Makes **200 ml (7 fl oz)**

150 g (5 oz) **papaya**
150 g (5 oz) **grapefruit**
150 g (5 oz) **raspberries**
juice of ½ **lime**, plus slices
   to serve (optional)
2–3 **ice cubes** (optional)

Scoop out the flesh of the papaya. Segment the grapefruit, leaving the pith on, and juice it with the papaya and raspberries and lime juice.

Pour into a glass, add the ice cubes, if using, and decorate with lime slices if liked.

For papaya & orange juice, replace the grapefruit and raspberries with the juice of 2 oranges and 125 g (4 oz) cucumber.

pineapple, grape & celery juice

Makes **200 ml (7 fl oz)**

125 g (4 oz) **pineapple**
125 g (4 oz) seedless **green grapes**
50 g (2 oz) **celery**
50 g (2 oz) **lettuce**, plus extra
  to serve (optional)
2–3 **ice cubes** (optional)

Remove the skin and core from the pineapple and roughly chop the flesh. Juice the pineapple with the grapes, celery and lettuce.

Pour the juice into a glass over ice, if using, decorate with pieces of lettuce, if liked, and serve immediately.

For pineapple & pear juice, double the amount of pineapple and replace the grapes, celery and lettuce with 2 pears and half a lime. This juice is rich in vitamins as well as being delicious.

celery, ginger & pineapple juice

Makes **200 ml (7 fl oz)**

125 g (4 oz) **celery**
125 g (4 oz) **pineapple**
2.5 cm (1 inch) piece **fresh
   root ginger**
crushed ice

Trim the celery and cut it into 5 cm (2 inch) lengths.
Remove the peel and core from the pineapple and chop
it into cubes. Peel and roughly chop the ginger. Juice the
celery with the pineapple and ginger.

Transfer the juice to a food processor or blender and
process with a little crushed ice. Pour into a glass and
serve immediately.

For pineapple & pink grapefruit juice, omit the celery
and ginger, double the amount of pineapple and juice it
with the flesh and skin of a pink grapefruit. Top up with
still water.

pineapple & alfalfa juice

Makes **250 ml (8 fl oz)**

150 g (5 oz) **pineapple**
150 g (5 oz) **alfalfa sprouts**,
  plus extra to decorate
2–3 **ice cubes**
50 ml (2 fl oz) **still water**

Peel and core the pineapple, chop the flesh into cubes and
juice.

Transfer the pineapple juice to a food processor or blender,
add the alfalfa sprouts, ice cubes and still water and
process briefly.

Pour the juice into a glass, sprinkle with extra alfalfa
sprouts and serve immediately.

For pineapple & lettuce juice, juice 125 g (4 oz)
pineapple with double the amount of lettuce. If you prefer
a really slushy drink, blend the resulting juice with some
ice cubes.

blackberry, cantaloupe melon & kiwifruit juice

Makes **250 ml (8 fl oz)**

100 g (3½ oz) **cantaloupe
  melon**
2 **kiwifruit**
100 (3½ oz) fresh or frozen
  blackberries, plus extra to
  decorate (optional)
2–3 **ice cubes**

Peel the melon and cut the flesh into cubes. Leaving on the skins, evenly slice the kiwifruit. Juice the melon and kiwifruit with the blackberries.

Transfer the juice to a food processor or blender and process with a couple of ice cubes. Pour into a glass and decorate with a few blackberries, if liked.

For melon & cherry juice, skin and roughly chop 300 g (10 oz) honeydew melon. Juice the melon flesh with 125 g (4 oz) pitted cherries.

blackberry, apple & celeriac juice

Makes **200 ml (7 fl oz)**

100 g (3½ oz) **celeriac**
50 g (2 oz) **apple**
100 g (3½ oz) frozen
  blackberries, plus extra
  to decorate
2–3 **ice cubes**

Peel the celeriac and cut the flesh into cubes. Roughly
chop the apple and juice it with the celeriac.

Transfer the juice to a food processor or blender, add the
blackberries and a couple of ice cubes and process briefly.

Pour the juice into a glass, decorate with extra blackberries
and serve immediately.

For blackberry & pineapple juice, juice 150 g (5 oz)
each of blackberries and pineapple with 25 g (1 oz) apple.
Serve in a tall glass over ice.

blueberry, apple & ginger juice

Makes **200 ml (7 fl oz)**

2.5 cm (1 inch) piece **fresh
   root ginger**, roughly
   chopped, plus extra to
   serve (optional)
250 g (8 oz) **blueberries**
125 g (4 oz) **grapefruit**
250 g (8 oz) **apples**
ice cubes (optional)

Peel and roughly chop the ginger. Juice the blueberries,
grapefruit and apple with the ginger.

Pour the juice into a glass over ice, if using, decorate with
thin slices of ginger, if liked, and serve immediately.

For apple & ginger juice, juice 250 g (8 oz) apple
with 2.5 cm (1 inch) ginger. If you like, top it up with
ice-cold water.

summer strawberry juice

Makes **200 ml (7 fl oz)**

100 g (3½ oz) **strawberries**
200 g (7 oz) **tomatoes**
basil leaves
ice cubes

Hull the strawberries. Juice the tomatoes with the strawberries and a few basil leaves, reserving 1 basil leaf for decoration.

Pour the juice into a glass over ice, decorate with the reserved basil leaf and serve immediately.

For strawberry & kiwifruit juice, wash and hull 150 g (5 oz) strawberries and juice them with 2 peeled kiwifruit.

apple, cranberry & blueberry juice

Makes **300 ml (10 fl oz)**

3 **apples**
150 ml (5 fl oz) unsweetened
  cranberry juice
125 g (4 oz) fresh or frozen
  blueberries
1 tablespoon **powdered**
  psyllium husks (optional)
ice cubes (optional)

Juice the apples. Transfer the apple juice to a food
processor or blender, add the cranberry juice, blueberries
and powdered psyllium husks, if using, and process.

Pour the juice into a glass over ice, if using, and serve
immediately.

For cranberry, apple & lettuce juice, juice half an apple
and 125 g (4 oz) lettuce with 50 g (2 oz) cranberries.
Serve over ice.

pear & cranberry juice

Makes **200 ml (7 fl oz)**

1 large **pear**
100 ml (3½ fl oz) **cranberry
   juice**
ice cubes

Juice the pear. Mix the pear juice with the cranberry juice.

Pour the combined juices into a glass over ice and serve immediately.

For cranberry & cucumber juice, use the same amount of cranberry juice and add the juice of 1 orange and 50 g (2 oz) cucumber.

orange & raspberry juice

Makes **500 ml (17 fl oz)**

2 large **oranges**
175 g (6 oz) **raspberries**
250 ml (8 fl oz) **still water**
ice cubes (optional)

Peel the oranges and divide the flesh into segments.
Juice the orange segments with the raspberries then add
the still water.

Pour the juice into 2 tall glasses over ice, if using, and
serve immediately.

For orange & apricot juice, juice 300 g (10 oz) fresh
apricots with 1 large orange. Top up with water to taste.

apple, mango & passionfruit juice

Makes **300 ml (½ pint)**

1 **mango**
2 **passionfruit**
3 **apples**, preferably red, plus
  extra to serve (optional)
ice cubes

Peel the mango and remove the stone. Slice the passionfruit in half, scoop out the flesh and discard the seeds. Juice the apples with the mango and passionfruit.

Pour the juice into a tall glass over ice, decorate with apple slices, if liked, and serve immediately.

For mango & pineapple juice, juice a peeled and stoned mango with 125 g (4 oz) pineapple and 3 apples. Top up with ice-cold water, if liked.

apple, apricot & peach juice

Makes **200 ml (7 fl oz)**

3 **apricots**
1 **peach**, plus extra to serve
  (optional)
2 **apples**
ice cubes

Halve and stone the apricots and peach. Juice the apples
with the apricots and peach.

Transfer the juice to a food processor or blender, add a few
ice cubes and process for 10 seconds.

Pour the juice into a glass, decorate with peach slices,
if liked, and serve immediately.

For apple & passionfruit juice, replace the peach with
2 passionfruit. Juice the apricot, apple and passionfruit and
serve over ice.

pear, kiwifruit & lime juice

Makes **300 ml (½ pint)**

3 **kiwifruit**, plus extra to serve
  (optional)
2 ripe **pears**
½ **lime**
2–3 **ice cubes** (optional)

Peel the kiwifruit. Slice the kiwifruit, pears and lime into even-sized pieces then juice.

Pour into a tall glass, add a couple of ice cubes, if using, decorate with slices of kiwifruit, if liked, and serve immediately.

For grape & kiwifruit juice, replace the pears and lime juice with 300 g (10 oz) seedless green grapes.

pear, celery & ginger juice

Makes **200 ml (7 fl oz)**

50 g (2 oz) **celery**
2.5 cm (1 inch) piece **fresh
  root ginger**
100 g (3½ oz) **pear**
ice cubes

Trim the celery and cut it into 5 cm (2 inch) lengths. Peel and roughly chop the ginger. Juice the pear with the celery and ginger.

Pour the juice into a glass over ice; alternatively, briefly process the juice in a food processor or blender with 2–3 ice cubes.

For pear & peach juice, juice 3 pears with 2 peaches to give a thick, nutritious drink.

pear, grapefruit & celery juice

Makes **200 ml (7 fl oz)**

75 g (3 oz) **grapefruit**
125 g (4 oz) **lettuce**
75 g (3 oz) **celery**
50 g (2 oz) **pear**
ice cubes (optional)

Peel the grapefruit and divide it into segments. Separate
the lettuce into leaves. Trim the celery and cut it into 5 cm
(2 inch) lengths. Quarter the pear. Juice the grapefruit with
the lettuce, celery and pear.

Pour the juice into a glass over ice, if using, and serve
immediately.

For grapefruit & lemon juice, peel and segment a
grapefruit and juice it with 5 cm (2 inches) cucumber and
half a lemon. Top up with sparkling mineral water.

grape & plum juice

Makes **300 ml** (½ **pint**)

about 300 g (10 oz) **plums**,
  plus extra to serve (optional)
150 g (5 oz) seedless **red
  grapes**
2–3 crushed **ice cubes**

Remove the stones from the plums then cut the flesh
into even-sized pieces. Juice with the grapes.

Pour the juice into a tall glass, add a couple of crushed ice
cubes, decorate with grapes or slices of plum, if liked,
and serve immediately.

For plum & orange juice, replace the grapes with
2 oranges. If you like, top up with sparkling mineral water.

grapefruit & orange juice

Makes **200 ml (7 fl oz)**

½ **grapefruit**
1 large **orange**
1 **lime**
ice cubes or **sparkling
  mineral water**

Peel all the fruit, leaving a little of the pith on the segments.
If you like, reserve some of the lime rind to decorate.

Juice the fruit, then either serve it over ice or, if you want
a longer drink, dilute it with an equal amount of sparkling
mineral water. Serve the juice decorated with curls of lime
rind, if liked.

For orange & carrot juice, peel and segment 2 oranges
and juice with 125 g (4 oz) carrots.

apricot & pineapple juice

Makes **350 ml (12 fl oz)**

65 g (2½ oz) ready-to-eat
  dried apricots
350 ml (12 fl oz) **pineapple
  juice**
2–3 **ice cubes**

Roughly chop the dried apricots and put them into a large
bowl. Pour over the pineapple juice, cover and leave to
stand overnight in the refrigerator.

Transfer the apricots and juice to a food processor or
blender and process until thick and smooth.

Pour the juice into a tall glass, add a couple of ice cubes
and serve immediately.

For dried apricot & orange juice, replace the pineapple
juice with the same quantity of orange juice; alternatively
juice 2 oranges with the apricots for a really fresh taste.

prune, pear & spinach juice

Makes **200 ml (7 fl oz)**

25 g (1 oz) ready-to-eat
  prunes
250 g (8 oz) **pear**, plus extra
  to serve (optional)
125 g (4 oz) **spinach**
ice cubes (optional)

Remove the stones from the prunes if necessary. Juice the pears and spinach with the prunes.

Pour the juice into a glass over ice, if using, decorate with slices of pear, if liked, and serve immediately.

For pear & avocado juice, roughly chop 375 g (12 oz) pears and blend with 75 g (3 oz) peeled and stoned avocados.

orange & passionfruit sparkler

Makes **200 ml (7 fl oz)**

100 g (3½ oz) **orange**
1 **passionfruit**
100 ml (3½ fl oz) **sparkling
  mineral water**
2–3 **ice cubes**

Peel, segment and juice the orange. Scoop the flesh out of
the passionfruit and press the pulp through a tea strainer to
extract the juice.

Mix the orange juice with the passionfruit juice and sparkling
water. Pour into a glass over ice and serve immediately.

For cherry cranberry fizz, juice 125 g (4 oz) pitted
cherries and 75 g (2 oz) cranberries and top up with
sparkling mineral water.

peach & ginger juice

Makes **200 ml (7 fl oz)**

250 g (8 oz) **peach**
2.5 cm (1 inch) piece **fresh
  root ginger**, roughly
  chopped
ice cubes
sparkling mineral water
mint leaves, to serve

Halve the peaches and remove the stones. Peel and roughly chop the ginger. Juice the peach with the ginger.

Pour the juice into a tall glass over ice, add a splash of sparkling mineral water and a couple of mint leaves and serve immediately.

For grapefruit fizz, juice 300 g (10 oz) grapefruit with 350 g (12 oz) cucumber and half a lemon. Top up with sparkling mineral water and stir in some chopped mint.

vegetable juices

broccoli, parsnip & apple juice

Makes **200 ml (7 fl oz)**

50 g (2 oz) **parsnip**
50 g (2 oz) **apple**
150 g (5 oz) **broccoli**
2–3 **ice cubes**

Peel the parsnip and cut the flesh into chunks. Quarter the apple and trim the broccoli. Juice the parsnip with the apple and broccoli.

Transfer the juice to a food processor or blender and process with the ice cubes to make a creamy juice.

Pour into a glass and serve immediately.

For broccoli, carrot & beetroot juice, trim 250 g (8 oz) broccoli and juice it with 175 g (6 oz) carrots and 50 g (2 oz) beetroot.

broccoli, spinach & tomato juice

Makes **200 ml (7 fl oz)**

150 g (5 oz) **spinach**
150 g (5 oz) **broccoli**
2 **tomatoes**
celery stick, to serve
   (optional)

Rinse the spinach and trim the broccoli. Juice the tomatoes with the green vegetables, adding the broccoli and spinach alternately so that the spinach leaves do not clog the juicer.

Pour the juice into a glass, add a stick of celery, if liked, and serve immediately.

For spinach & carrot juice, rinse 250 g (8 oz) spinach and juice the leaves with 250 g (8 oz) carrots and 25 g (1 oz) parsley. Stir in a teaspoon of spirulina, the freshwater algae supplement, for extra energy.

broccoli, spinach & apple juice

Makes **200 ml (7 fl oz)**

150 g (5 oz) **broccoli**
150 g (5 oz) **spinach**
2 **apples**
2–3 **ice cubes**

Trim the broccoli and rinse the spinach. Juice the apples with the spinach and broccoli, alternating the spinach leaves with the other ingredients so that the spinach leaves do not clog the machine.

Transfer the juice to a food processor or blender, add a couple of ice cubes and process briefly.

Pour into a glass and serve immediately.

For spinach, apple & pepper juice, increase the apple to 250 g (8 oz) and, instead of broccoli, juice 100 g (3½ oz) yellow pepper. Stir in a pinch of ground cinnamon before serving.

broccoli & kale juice

Makes **200 ml (7 fl oz)**

100 g (3½ oz) **broccoli**
100 g (3½ oz) **kale**
50 g (2 oz) **celery**
25 g (1 oz) **parsley**
200 g (7 oz) **apple**
ice cubes

Trim the broccoli and kale. Trim the celery and cut it into 5 cm (2 inch) lengths. Juice the parsley and apple with the broccoli, kale and celery.

Pour the juice into a glass over ice and serve immediately.

For broccoli, lettuce & celery juice, trim 150 g (5 oz) broccoli and juice it with 100 g (3½ oz) lettuce and the same amount of celery.

celeriac, alfalfa & orange juice

Makes **200 ml (7 fl oz)**

100 g (3½ oz) **orange**, plus
  extra to serve (optional)
100 g (3½ oz) **celeriac**
100 g (3½ oz) **alfalfa sprouts**

Peel the orange and separate it into segments. Peel the celeriac and cut it into chunks. Rinse the alfalfa sprouts. Juice the ingredients.

Pour the juice into a glass, add slices of orange, if liked, and serve immediately.

For celery, alfalfa & apple juice, trim 3 celery sticks and cut them into 5 cm (2 inch) lengths. Juice them with 2 apples and 25 g (1 oz) alfalfa sprouts. This juice is delicious served ice cold.

tomato, red pepper & papaya juice

Makes **200 ml (7 fl oz)**

about 125 g (4 oz) **papaya**
about 100 g (3½ oz) **red**
 pepper
1 large **tomato**
2–3 **ice cubes**

Peel and deseed the papaya. Core and deseed the pepper. Juice the tomato with the papaya and pepper.

Transfer the juice to a food processor or blender, add a couple of ice cubes and process.

Pour the juice into a glass and serve immediately.

For pepper & orange juice, core and deseed 100 g (3½ oz) each of red, yellow and orange peppers and juice the pepper flesh with 1 orange. Serve sprinkled with chopped mint.

tomato, carrot & ginger juice

Makes **150 ml** (¼ **pint)**

2.5 cm (1 inch) cube **fresh
  root ginger**
100 g (3½ oz) **celery**, plus
  extra to serve (optional)
300 g (10 oz) **tomatoes**
175 g (6 oz) **carrot**
1 **garlic clove**
2.5 cm (1 inch) piece fresh
  horseradish
2–3 **ice cubes**

Peel and roughly chop the ginger. Trim the celery and cut it into 5 cm (2 inch) lengths. Juice the tomatoes, carrot, garlic and horseradish with the ginger and celery.

Transfer the juice to a food processor or blender, add a couple of ice cubes and process briefly.

Pour the juice into a small glass, garnish with celery slivers, if liked, and serve immediately.

For carrot & pink grapefruit juice, peel and segment a pink grapefruit, leaving some pith, and juice with 2 carrots and 2 apples. Serve topped up with mineral water.

tomato, red pepper & cabbage juice

Makes **200 ml (7 fl oz)**

175 g (6 oz) **red pepper**
175 g (6 oz) **tomatoes**
100 g (3½ oz) **white cabbage**
1 tablespoon chopped
   parsley
lime wedge, to decorate
   (optional)

Core and deseed the pepper. Juice the tomatoes and cabbage with the pepper.

Pour the juice into a tall glass, stir in the parsley, decorate with a lime wedge, if liked, and serve immediately.

For tomato, red pepper & celery juice, trim 4 celery sticks and cut them into 5 cm (2 inch) lengths. Juice the celery with 3 ripe tomatoes and half a red pepper. Add a crushed garlic clove and chopped chilli, to taste.

tomato, lemon & parsley juice

Makes **300 ml (½ pint)**

2 **celery sticks**, plus leaves
   to serve (optional)
4 **tomatoes**
large handful of **parsley**
rind and juice of ½ **lemon**
ice cubes

Trim the celery sticks and cut them into 5 cm (2 inch) lengths. Juice the tomatoes and parsley with the celery, lemon juice and rind.

Pour the juice into a tall glass over ice, add the celery leaves, if using, and serve immediately.

For tomato & celery juice, replace the lemon juice and rind and the parsley with Tabasco sauce, celery salt and black pepper, to taste.

tomato, apple & basil juice

Makes **200 ml (7 fl oz)**

1 **celery stick**
4 large **tomatoes**
1 **apple**
ice cubes
4 **basil leaves**, finely chopped
1½ tablespoons **lime juice**
extra **basil leaves,** to serve
(optional)

Trim the celery and cut it into 5 cm (2 inch) lengths. Juice the tomatoes and apple with the celery.

Pour the juice into a glass over ice, stir in the basil leaves and lime juice, shred extra basil leaves and add, if liked, and serve immediately.

For tomato, cauliflower & carrot juice, trim 100 g (3½ oz) cauliflower and juice with 1 large tomato and 200 g (7 oz) carrot.

celery & celeriac juice

Makes **250 ml (8 fl oz)**

100 g (3½ oz) **celery**
150 g (5 oz) **celeriac**
100 g (3½ oz) **lettuce**
100 g (3½ oz) **spinach**
2–3 **ice cubes**

Trim the celery and cut it into 5 cm (2 inch) lengths. Peel the celeriac and cut the flesh into cubes. Separate the lettuce into leaves. Juice the celery, celeriac, lettuce and spinach, alternating the ingredients so that the lettuce and spinach leaves do not clog the machine.

Transfer the juice to a food processor or blender, add a couple of ice cubes and process briefly.

Pour the juice into a tall glass and serve immediately.

For carrot, celery & celeriac juice, peel 125 g (4 oz) celeriac and trim and cut 4 celery stalks into 5 cm (2 inch) lengths. Juice the celeriac and celery with 1 carrot.

carrot, beetroot & sweet potato juice

Makes **200 ml (7 fl oz)**

175 g (6 oz) **sweet potato**
  or **yam**
100 g (3½ oz) **beetroot**
175 g (6 oz) **carrot**
125 g (4 oz) **fennel**
ice cubes
fennel fronds, to decorate
  (optional)

Peel the sweet potato or yam and scrub the beetroot. Juice the carrot and fennel with the sweet potato and beetroot.

Pour the juice into a glass over ice, decorate with fennel fronds, if liked, and serve immediately.

For carrot, beetroot & orange juice, replace the sweet potato and fennel with 125 g (4 oz) strawberries and 1 orange. This colourful juice will give you an instant energy boost.

carrot, cabbage & apple juice

Makes **200 ml (7 fl oz)**

175 g (6 oz) **carrot**
250 g (8 oz) **apple**
125 g (4 oz) **red cabbage**
orange slices, to decorate
ice cubes

Roughly chop the carrot and apple and juice them with the cabbage.

Pour the juice into a glass over ice, decorate with a slice of orange, and serve immediately.

For carrot, spinach & pink grapefruit juice, juice 125 g (4 oz) each of carrot, spinach and pink grapefruit. This juice has a pleasantly astringent flavour.

carrot, fennel & ginger juice

Makes **200 ml (7 fl oz)**

2.5 cm (1 inch) piece **fresh
  root ginger**
75 g (3 oz) **celery**
300 g (10 oz) **carrot**
50 g (2 oz) **fennel**, plus extra
  to serve (optional)
1 tablespoon **spirulina**
  (optional)
ice cubes (optional)
fennel fronds, to decorate
  (optional)

Peel and roughly chop the ginger. Trim the celery and cut
it into 5 cm (2 inch) lengths. Juice the carrot, fennel and
spirulina, if using, with the ginger and celery.

Pour the juice into a glass over ice, if using, decorate
with strips of fennel and fennel fronds, if liked, and serve
immediately.

For carrot, apple & ginger juice, peel and roughly chop
1 cm (½ inch) cube fresh root ginger and juice it with
2 carrots and 1 tart apple, such as a Granny Smith.

carrot & lettuce juice

Makes **200 ml (7 fl oz)**

100 g (3½ oz) **carrot**
200 g (7 oz) **lettuce**
ice cubes
chopped **coriander leaves**,
   to decorate

Chop the carrot into chunks and separate the lettuce leaves. Juice the carrot with the lettuce, taking care that the lettuce leaves do not clog the machine.

Pour the juice into a glass over ice, decorate with chopped coriander and serve immediately.

For carrot & green leaf juice, add 90 g (3 oz) celery, 100 g (3½ oz) spinach and 25 g (1 oz) parsley to the carrot and lettuce.

carrot & kiwifruit juice

Makes **250 ml (8 fl oz)**

about 200 g (7 oz) **carrot**
1 **kiwifruit**, plus extra to serve
  (optional)
ice cubes (optional)

Cut the carrot and kiwifruit into even-sized pieces and juice together.

Pour the juice into a glass over ice, if using, decorate with slices of kiwifruit, if liked, and serve immediately.

For cucumber & kiwifruit juice, omit the carrots and instead juice 1½ cucumbers with the kiwifruit. Serve with a squeeze of lemon.

carrot, parsnip & sweet potato juice

Makes **200 ml (7 fl oz)**

175 g (6 oz) **celery**
175 g (6 oz) **carrot**
175 g (6 oz) **parsnip**
175 g (6 oz) **sweet potato**
handful of **parsley**, plus extra
  to serve (optional)
1 **garlic clove**
2–3 **ice cubes**
lemon wedge

Trim the celery and cut it into 5 cm (2 inch) lengths. Juice the carrot, parsnip, sweet potato, parsley and garlic with the celery.

Transfer the juice to a food processor or blender and process with a couple of ice cubes.

Pour the juice into a glass, decorate with a wedge of lemon and a parsley sprig, if liked, and serve immediately.

For carrot, parsnip & melon juice, which is especially rich in folic acid, juice 125 g (4 oz) each of carrot, parsnip, lettuce and cantaloupe melon.

carrot, radish & cucumber juice

Makes **200 ml (7 fl oz)**

100 g (3½ oz) **potato**
100 g (3½ oz) **radish**, plus
  extra to serve (optional)
100 g (3½ oz) **carrot**
100 g (3½ oz) **cucumber**
ice cubes

Juice the potato, radish, carrot and cucumber.

Transfer the juice to a food processor or blender, add a
couple of ice cubes and process briefly.

Pour the juice into a tall glass over ice, decorate with slices
of radish, if liked, and serve immediately.

For carrot, radish & ginger juice, omit the potato and
cucumber and add 2.5 cm (1 inch) peeled and roughly
chopped fresh root ginger. This is a good juice if you have
a cold or blocked sinuses.

carrot, chilli & pineapple juice

Makes **200 ml (7 fl oz)**

½ small **chilli**
250 g (8 oz) **pineapple**
250 g (8 oz) **carrot**
ice cubes
juice of ½ **lime**
1 tablespoon chopped
   coriander leaves

Deseed the chilli. Remove the core and peel from the pineapple. Juice the carrots with the chilli and pineapple.

Pour the juice into a glass over ice. Squeeze over the lime juice, stir in the chopped coriander and serve immediately.

For tomato, celery & ginger juice, trim 100 g (3½ oz) celery and roughly chop 2.5 cm (1 inch) piece each of fresh root ginger and fresh horseradish. Juice the celery, ginger and horseradish with 300 g (10 oz) tomatoes, 175 g (6 oz) carrot and a garlic clove. Serve over ice, decorated with celery slivers, if liked.

carrot, chicory & celery juice

Makes **200 ml (7 fl oz)**

175 g (6 oz) **carrot**
125 g (4 oz) **celery**
125 g (4 oz) **chicory**
2–3 **ice cubes**
lemon slices, to serve
chopped **parsley**, to serve
   (optional)

Scrub the carrots. Trim the celery and cut it into 5 cm (2 inch) lengths. Juice the chicory with the carrot and the celery.

Transfer the juice to a food processor or blender, add a couple of ice cubes and process briefly.

Pour the juice into a glass, decorate with slices of lemon and some chopped parsley, if liked, and serve immediately.

For carrot & cabbage juice, juice 250 g (8 oz) each of carrot and cabbage and serve over ice. This quick juice soothes upset stomachs.

parsnip, green pepper & watercress juice

Makes **200 ml (7 fl oz)**

175 g (6 oz) **green pepper**
100 g (3½ oz) **watercress**
175 g (6 oz) **cucumber**
175 g (6 oz) **parsnip**
ice cubes
chopped **mint**, to decorate

Core and deseed the pepper. Juice the watercress and cucumber with the parsnip and peppers.

Pour the juice into a tall glass over ice, decorate with a sprinkling of mint and serve immediately.

For watercress & pear juice, juice 40 g (1½ oz) watercress with 3 ripe pears. This simple juice is highly nutritious.

seven vegetable juice

Makes **200 ml (7 fl oz)**

50 g (2 oz) **green pepper**
50 g (2 oz) **celery**
90 g (3 oz) **carrot**
25 g (1 oz) **spinach**
25 g (1 oz) **onion**
90 g (3 oz) **cucumber**
50 g (2 oz) **tomatoes**, plus
  extra to serve (optional)
sea salt and pepper

Core and deseed the pepper. Trim the celery and cut it into
5 cm (2 inch) lengths. Juice the carrot, spinach, onion,
cucumber and tomato with the pepper and celery, taking
care that the spinach leaves do not clog the machine.

Pour the juice into a glass and season with sea salt and
black pepper. Decorate with tomato quarters, if liked, and
serve immediately.

For yellow pepper, spinach & apple juice, core and
deseed 100 g (3½ oz) yellow pepper and juice the flesh
with 125 g (4 oz) spinach and 250 g (8 oz) apple.

cabbage, apple & cinnamon juice

Makes **200 ml (7 fl oz)**

200 g (7 oz) **green cabbage**
50 g (2 oz) **apple**
2–3 **ice cubes**
ground cinnamon, plus extra
   to decorate

Separate the cabbage into leaves and cut the apple into pieces. Juice the cabbage with the apple.

Transfer the juice to a food processor or blender, add a couple of ice cubes and a sprinkling of cinnamon and process briefly.

Pour the juice into a glass, decorate with a sprinkling of cinnamon and serve immediately.

For red cabbage, grape & orange juice, juice 125 g (4 oz) red cabbage with half an orange and a handful of seedless red grapes to make a colourful and only slightly sweet drink.

cabbage & pear juice

Makes **200 ml (7 fl oz)**

125 g (4 oz) **cabbage**
50 g (2 oz) **celery**
25 g (1 oz) **watercress**
250 g (8 oz) **pear**
ice cubes (optional)
1 **celery stick**, to serve
   (optional)

Chop the cabbage roughly. Trim the celery and cut it into
5 cm (2 inch) lengths. Juice the watercress with the pears,
cabbage and celery.

Pour the juice into a tall glass over ice, if using, and serve
immediately with a short celery stick, if liked.

For fennel, celery & grapefruit juice, juice 100 g
(3½ oz) each of celery and fennel with ½ a grapefruit.
Serve with ice.

spinach, celery & cucumber juice

Makes **200 ml (7 fl oz)**

50 g (2 oz) **green pepper**
50 g (2 oz) **celery**
25 g (1 oz) **spinach**
100 g (3½ oz) **cucumber**
100 g (3½ oz) **tomatoes**, plus
  extra to serve (optional)
salt and pepper
ice cubes (optional)

Core and deseed the pepper. Trim the celery and cut it into 5 cm (2 inch) lengths. Juice the spinach, cucumber and tomatoes with the pepper and celery. Season the juice to taste with salt and pepper.

Pour the juice into a glass over ice, if using, decorate with tomato quarters, if liked, and serve immediately.

For kale & spirulina juice, juice 25 g (1 oz) kale with 100 g (3½ oz) wheatgrass. Stir in 1 teaspoon spirulina before serving. This unusual-tasting juice offers excellent health benefits.

lettuce, grape & ginger juice

Makes **200 ml (7 fl oz)**

2.5 cm (1 inch) piece **fresh
root ginger**, chopped
200 g (7 oz) seedless **green
grapes**, plus extra to
decorate (optional)
200 g (7 oz) **lettuce**
ice cubes (optional)

Peel and roughly chop the ginger. Juice the grapes and
lettuce with the ginger, alternating the ingredients so that
the lettuce leaves do not clog the machine.

Pour the juice into a glass, decorate with a few grapes, if
liked, and serve immediately. Alternatively, for a creamier
drink, transfer the juice to a food processor or blender, add
a couple of ice cubes and process briefly.

For lettuce & apple juice, juice 175 g (6 oz) Cos
(romaine) lettuce with 1 large apple, making sure that the
lettuce leaves do not clog the machine.

fennel & camomile juice

Makes **200 ml (7 fl oz)**

1 **lemon**, plus extra to serve
  (optional)
150 g (5 oz) **fennel**
100 ml (3½ fl oz) chilled
  camomile tea
ice cubes

Peel the lemon and juice it with the fennel. Mix the juice with the camomile tea.

Pour the juice into a glass over ice and serve with slices of lemon, if liked.

For fennel & lettuce juice, juice 125 g (4 oz) fennel and 175 g (6 oz) lettuce with half a lemon. Serve with ice and a slice of lemon.

lettuce & kiwifruit juice

Makes **200 ml (7 fl oz)**

100 g (3½ oz) **kiwifruit**, plus
   extra to serve (optional)
200 g (7 oz) **lettuce**
ice cubes (optional)

Peel the kiwifruit and roughly chop the flesh. Separate
the lettuce into leaves. Juice the kiwifruit and lettuce,
alternating the ingredients so that the lettuce leaves
do not clog the machine.

Pour the juice into a glass over ice, if using, decorate with
slices of kiwifruit, if liked, and serve immediately.

For lettuce & camomile juice, juice half a lemon with
200 g (7 oz) lettuce. Mix the juice with 100 ml (3½ fl oz)
chilled camomile tea and serve with a couple of ice cubes
and a slice of lemon.

red onion & beetroot juice

Makes **200 ml (7 fl oz)**

125 g (4 oz) **watercress**
125 g (4 oz) **red onion**
1 **garlic clove**
250 g (8 oz) **carrot**
125 g (4 oz) **beetroot**, plus
   leaves to serve (optional)

Juice the watercress, onion and garlic with the carrot
and beetroot.

Pour the juice into a glass, decorate with beetroot leaves,
if liked, and serve immediately.

For carrot & beetroot juice, peel and roughly chop
2.5 cm (1 inch) cube fresh root ginger and juice the ginger
with 10 large carrots with 4 large beetroots. Serve over ice.

jerusalem artichoke, celery & celeriac juice

Makes **200 ml (7 fl oz)**

100 g (3½ oz) **celeriac**
100 g (3½ oz) **Jerusalem
  artichokes**
100 g (3½ oz) **celery**
small bunch of **mint**
2–3 **ice cubes**

Peel the celeriac and chop the flesh into sticks. Juice with the Jerusalem artichokes, celery and the mint, alternating the mint leaves with the other ingredients to make sure that the leaves do not clog the machine.

Transfer the juice to a food processor or blender, add a couple of ice cubes and process briefly.

Pour the juice into a glass and serve immediately.

For Jerusalem artichoke & carrot juice, juice 100 g (3½ oz) each of artichokes, carrots, lettuce, Brussels sprouts and green beans with half a lemon.

healthy
smoothies

cucumber, lemon & mint smoothie

Makes **300 ml (½ pint)**

250 g (8 oz) **cucumber**, plus
  extra to serve
½ **lemon**
3–4 fresh **mint leaves**
2–3 **ice cubes**

Peel and roughly chop the cucumber. Squeeze the lemon.

Put the cucumber and lemon into a food processor or blender with the mint leaves and ice cubes and process briefly.

Pour the smoothie into a tall glass, decorate with a strip of cucumber, if liked, and serve immediately.

For grapefruit & cucumber crush, chop 1 cucumber and blend it with 150 ml (¼ pint) grapefruit juice and a handful of ice cubes. Process the ingredients to make an ice-cold slushy drink.

cucumber lassi

Makes **400 ml (14 fl oz)**

150 g (5 oz) **cucumber**
150 g (5 oz) live **natural
  yogurt**
100 ml (3½ fl oz) ice-cold
  still water
handful of **mint**
½ teaspoon **ground cumin**
squeeze of **lemon juice**

Peel and roughly chop the cucumber. Place in a food
processor or blender and add the yogurt and iced water.

Pull the mint leaves off their stalks, reserving a few for
decoration. Chop the remainder roughly and put them into
the food processor. Add the cumin and lemon juice and
process briefly.

Pour the smoothie into a tall glass, decorate with mint
leaves, if liked, and serve immediately.

For mango lassi, cut the flesh of a mango into cubes and
add it to a food processor or blender with 150 ml (¼ pint)
live natural yogurt and the same amount of ice-cold still
water, 1 tablespoon rosewater and ¼ teaspoon ground
cardamom. Process briefly and serve.

cranberry & yogurt smoothie

Makes **300 ml (½ pint)**

100 g (3½ oz) **cranberries**
50 g (2 oz) **Greek yogurt**
100 ml (3½ fl oz) **soya milk**
2–3 **ice cubes**
artificial sweetener, to taste

Put the cranberries in a food processor or blender, add the yogurt, soya milk and ice cubes and process.

Taste and add artificial sweetener if required. Process once again.

Pour the smoothie into a large glass and serve immediately.

For raspberry shake, put 150 ml (¼ pint) soya milk and 100 g (3½ oz) frozen raspberries in a food processor or blender and process until smooth.

cranberry & apple smoothie

Makes **200 ml (7 fl oz)**

250 g (8 oz) **apple**
100 g (3½ oz) frozen
  cranberries
100 g (3½ oz) live **natural**
  yogurt
1 tablespoon **clear honey**
ice cubes (optional)

Juice the apples.

Transfer the juice to a food processor or blender, add
the cranberries, yogurt and honey and process briefly.

Pour the smoothie into a glass over ice, if using, and
serve immediately.

For grapeberry smoothie, blend together 125 g (4 oz)
blackberries, 300 ml (½ pint) purple grape juice and
3 tablespoons live natural yogurt.

mandarin & lychee frappé

Makes **150 ml (¼ pint)**

100 g (3½ oz) **mandarin
  oranges**, canned in natural
  juice
50 g (2 oz) **lychees**, canned
  in natural juice
ice cubes

Put the oranges and lychees and the juices from the cans
into a food processor or blender, add the ice cubes and
process briefly.

Pour the frappé into a glass and serve immediately.

For ruby smoothie, put the juice of 2 oranges and
1 apple in a food processor or blender with 150 g (5 oz)
each raspberries and strawberries. Add 150 ml (¼ pint)
live natural yogurt and process briefly.

orange super-smoothie

Makes **200 ml (7 fl oz)**

1 large **carrot**
1 **orange**
100 g (3½ oz) **banana**
1 fresh or dried **apricot**
2–3 **ice cubes**

Juice the carrot and orange together.

Transfer the juice to a food processor or blender, add the banana, apricot and a couple of ice cubes and blend briefly.

Pour the smoothie into a glass and serve immediately.

For orange & banana smoothie, which makes a great breakfast or lunch, place 1 banana, 150 ml (¼ pint) fresh orange juice and 25 g (1 oz) sunflower seeds in a food processor or blender and blend together.

orange, mango & strawberry smoothie

Makes **400 ml (14 fl oz)**

125 g (4 oz) **strawberries**
1 small ripe **mango**
300 ml (½ pint) **orange juice**
orange slices, to decorate
  (optional)

Hull the strawberries, put them in a freezer container and freeze for 2 hours or overnight.

Peel the mango, remove the stone, roughly chop the flesh and put it in a food processor or blender with the strawberries and orange juice and process until thick.

Pour the smoothie into a tall glass, decorate with slices of orange, if liked, and serve immediately.

For orange & banana smoothie, blend a ripe banana with the strawberries and orange juice. Serve decorated with orange slices, if liked.

banana & peanut butter smoothie

Makes **400 ml (14 fl oz)**

1 ripe **banana**
300 ml (½ pint) **semi-skimmed milk**
1 tablespoon smooth **peanut butter** or 2 teaspoons **tahini paste**

Peel and slice the banana, put it in a freezer container and freeze for at least 2 hours or overnight.

Put the banana, milk and peanut butter or tahini paste in a food processor or blender and process until smooth.

Pour the smoothie into a tall glass and serve immediately.

For banana almond smoothie, put 2 frozen bananas, 450 ml (¾ pint) soya milk, 40 g (1½ oz) ground almonds and a pinch of cinnamon into a food processor or blender and process briefly.

banana, orange & mango smoothie

Makes **500 ml (17 fl oz)**

1 ripe **banana**
1 ripe **mango**
200 ml (7 fl oz) **orange juice**
200 ml (7 fl oz) **semi-
   skimmed milk**
3 tablespoons **fromage frais**
ice cubes (optional)

Peel and slice the banana. Peel the mango, remove the stone and cut the flesh into even-sized pieces.

Put the banana and mango in a food processor or blender, add the orange juice, milk and fromage frais and process until smooth.

Pour the smoothie into 2 glasses over ice, if using, and serve immediately.

For banana & avocado smoothie, process 1 small ripe banana with 1 small ripe avocado and 250 ml (8 fl oz) skimmed milk.

banana & fig smoothie

Makes **200 ml (7 fl oz)**

2.5 cm (1 inch) piece **fresh
  root ginger**
100 g (3½ oz) **fig**, plus extra
  to serve (optional)
1 **orange**
250 g (8 oz) **carrot**
100 g (3½ oz) **banana**
ice cubes

Peel and roughly chop the ginger. Juice the fig and orange
with the carrot and ginger.

Transfer the juice to a food processor or blender, add
the banana and some ice cubes and process until smooth.

Pour the drink into a glass, add more ice cubes, decorate
with sliced figs, if liked, and serve immediately.

For banana & papaya smoothie, put the flesh of a
papaya in a food processor or blender with a banana, the
juice of 1 orange, 300 ml (½ pint) apple juice and some
ice. Process until smooth.

prune, apple & cinnamon smoothie

Makes **400 ml (14 fl oz)**

65 g (2½ oz) ready-to-eat
 prunes
pinch of **ground cinnamon**,
 plus extra to serve
350 ml (12 fl oz) **apple juice**
3 tablespoons **Greek yogurt**
ice cubes

Roughly chop the prunes. Put the prunes and cinnamon in a large bowl, pour over the apple juice, cover and leave to stand overnight.

Put the prunes, apple juice and yogurt in a food processor or blender and process until smooth.

Pour the smoothie into a large glass over ice cubes, sprinkle with extra cinnamon and drink immediately.

For apple & avocado smoothie, process the flesh of a small, ripe avocado with 100 ml (3½ fl oz) apple juice.

apple, banana & wheatgerm smoothie

Makes **1 litre (1¾ pints)**

2 tablespoons **wheatgerm**
1 tablespoon **sesame seeds**
2 **bananas**
75 g (3 oz) **pineapple**
450 ml (¾ pint) **apple juice**
300 ml (½ pint) **live natural yogurt**

Spread the wheatgerm and sesame seeds over a baking sheet and toast gently under a preheated grill, stirring a couple of times until the sesame seeds have begun to turn a golden brown. Remove from the grill and leave to cool.

Peel and slice the bananas. Remove the skin and core from the pineapple and chop the flesh. Put the banana and pineapple in a food processor or blender and process to a rough purée.

Add the apple juice and blend again to make a smooth juice. Add the yogurt and the cooled wheatgerm and sesame seeds. Blend again.

Pour the smoothie into a jug and serve immediately in glasses.

For apple & oat smoothie, process an apple and a banana with 150 g (5 oz) plain live yogurt, 200 ml (7 fl oz) skimmed milk, a few drops of vanilla extract, 2 teaspoons clear honey and 2 tablespoons muesli in a food processor or blender.

summer berry smoothie

Makes **400 ml (14 fl oz)**

150 g (5 oz) frozen **mixed
  summer berries**, plus extra
  to serve (optional)
300 ml (½ pint) **vanilla-
  flavoured soya milk**
1 teaspoon **clear honey**
  (optional)

Put the berries, soya milk and honey, if using, in a food
processor or blender and process until thick.

Pour the smoothie into 2 short glasses, decorate with
berries, if liked, and serve immediately.

For blueberry & grape smoothie, blend together
125 g (4 oz) frozen blueberries, 250 g (8 oz) red grapes
and 3 tablespoons fromage frais.

blueberry & mint smoothie

Makes **250 ml (8 fl oz)**

100 g (3½ oz) frozen
  blueberries
150 ml (¼ pint) **soya milk**
small bunch of **mint**

Put the blueberries in a food processor or blender and pour in the soya milk. Pull the mint leaves off their stalks, reserving one or two sprigs for decoration, and add the remainder to the blender. Process briefly.

Pour the smoothie into a glass, decorate with the reserved mint sprigs and serve immediately.

For blueberry & apple smoothie, process 250 g (8 oz) apples with 125 g (4 oz) blueberries in a food processor or blender until smooth.

beetroot & berry smoothie

Makes **250 ml (8 fl oz)**

50 g (2 oz) **beetroot**
100 g (3½ oz) **blueberries**,
  plus extra to serve (optional)
100 g (3½ oz) **raspberries**
2–3 **ice cubes**

Juice the beetroot.

Pour the beetroot juice into a food processor or blender, add the blueberries, raspberries and ice cubes and process until smooth.

Pour the mixture into a glass, decorate with blueberries, if liked, and serve immediately.

For blueberry & grapefruit smoothie, juice 125 g (4 oz) grapefruit with 250 g (8 oz) apples. Transfer the juice to a food processor or blender with 125 g (4 oz) blueberries and 2.5 cm (1 inch) piece fresh root ginger and process until smooth.

raspberry, kiwifruit & grapefruit smoothie

Makes **200 ml (7 fl oz)**

150 g (5 oz) **grapefruit**
175 g (6 oz) **pineapple**
50 g (2 oz) **kiwifruit**
50 g (2 oz) frozen
  raspberries, plus extra
  to serve (optional)
50 g (2 oz) frozen **cranberries**

Peel and segment the grapefruit. Remove the skin and core from the pineapple. Juice the kiwifruit with the grapefruit and pineapple.

Transfer the juice to a food processor or blender, add the frozen berries and process until smooth.

Pour the smoothie into a glass, decorate with raspberries, if liked, and serve with a straw.

For strawberry & pineapple smoothie, process 150 g (5 oz) frozen strawberries with 150 ml (¼ pint) pineapple juice and 150 g (5 oz) strawberry yogurt.

strawberry lassi

Makes **1.5 litres (2½ pints)**

400 g (13 oz) **strawberries**
750 ml (1¼ pints) **ice-cold
  water**
300 ml (½ pint) **low-fat live
  natural yogurt**
25 g (1 oz) **golden caster
  sugar**
few drops of **rosewater**
coarsely ground **black
  pepper**, to serve

Hull and roughly chop the strawberries. Put the strawberries in a food processor or blender with half the water and process until smooth.

Add the yogurt, sugar, rosewater and the remaining water and process again until smooth and frothy.

Pour the smoothie into chilled glasses, sprinkle with black pepper and serve immediately.

For banana lassi, process 2 small ripe bananas with 300 ml (½ pint) live natural yogurt, 125 ml (4 fl oz) ice-cold water and a pinch of ground cardamom in a food processor or blender.

mango, pineapple & lime smoothie

Makes **400 ml (14 fl oz)**

1 ripe **mango**
300 ml (½ pint) **pineapple**
  juice
rind and juice of ½ **lime**
lime wedges, to serve
  (optional)

Peel the mango, remove the stone, roughly chop the flesh
and put it in a freezer container. Freeze for at least 2 hours
or overnight.

Put the frozen mango in a food processor or blender, add
the pineapple juice and lime rind and juice and process
until thick.

Pour the smoothie into 2 short glasses, decorate with lime
wedges, if liked, and serve immediately.

For apricot & pineapple smoothie, soak 65 g (2½ oz)
dried apricots overnight in 350 ml (12 fl oz) pineapple
juice. Process the mixture in a food processor or blender
with some ice until smooth.

mango & mint sherbet

Makes **1.5 litres (2½ pints)**

3 ripe **mangoes**
4 tablespoons **lemon juice**
1 tablespoon **caster sugar**
12 **mint leaves**, finely
  chopped
900 ml (1½ pints) ice-cold
  water
ice cubes

Peel and stone the mangoes and roughly chop the flesh.
Put it into a food processor or blender with the lemon juice,
sugar, mint leaves and water and process until smooth.

Pour the smoothie into tall glasses over ice and serve
immediately.

For mango & blackcurrant smoothie, process the flesh
of 3 mangoes with 100 ml (3½ fl oz) apple juice
and 200 g (7 oz) blackcurrants.

mango, coconut & lime lassi

Makes **600 ml (1 pint)**

1 large ripe **mango**
juice of 1 **orange**
juice of 1 **lime**
1 tablespoon **clear honey**
300 g (10 oz) **natural yogurt**
4 tablespoons **coconut milk**
orange slices, to decorate
  (optional)
ice cubes (optional)

Peel the mango, remove the stone and dice the flesh. Put the mango in a food processor or blender with the orange and lime juices, honey, yogurt and coconut milk. Process until smooth.

Transfer the mixture to a jug then pour into tall glasses over ice, if using, decorate with slices of orange, if liked, and serve immediately.

For pineapple & coconut smoothie, process 100 g (3½ oz) pineapple flesh with 100 ml (3½ fl oz) coconut milk and 100 ml (3½ fl oz) soya milk. Serve sprinkled with toasted coconut.

tropical fruit smoothie

Makes **600 ml (1 pint)**

1 large **banana**
1 large ripe **mango**
150 g (5 oz) **natural yogurt**
300 ml (½ pint) **pineapple juice**
pineapple chunks, to serve
  (optional)

Peel and slice the banana, then put it in a freezer-proof container and freeze for at least 2 hours or overnight.

Peel the mango, remove the stone and roughly chop the flesh. Place the flesh in a food processor or blender with the frozen banana, yogurt and pineapple juice and process until smooth.

Pour the mixture into tall glasses, decorate with pineapple chunks, if liked, and serve immediately.

For kiwifruit, melon & passionfruit smoothie, freeze 300 g (10 oz) watermelon flesh, then blend it with 2 kiwifruit and add 200 ml (7 fl oz) passionfruit juice.

peach & tofu smoothie

Makes **300 ml (½ pint)**

100 g (3½ oz) **peach**
100 g (3½ oz) **tofu**
50 g (2 oz) **vanilla ice cream**
100 ml (3½ fl oz) **still water**
few drops of natural **almond
   essence**
ice cubes (optional)

Halve the peach, remove the skin and stone and roughly chop the peach flesh.

Put the peach in a food processor or blender and add the tofu and ice cream. Pour in the water, add a little almond essence and process until smooth.

Pour the mixture into 2 short glasses over ice, if using, and serve immediately.

For rhubarb smoothie, blend 100 g (3½ oz) stewed rhubarb with 100 g (3½ oz) plain live yogurt and 2 drops of vanilla extract. Sweeten to taste with honey.

peach & orange smoothie

Makes **200 ml (7 fl oz)**

200 g (7 oz) **peaches,**
   canned in natural juice
75 ml (3 fl oz) **peach- or**
   apricot-flavoured yogurt,
   plus extra to serve
100 ml (3½ fl oz) **orange juice**
1 teaspoon **clear honey**
   (optional)
ice cubes (optional)

Drain the peaches and discard the juice.

Put the peaches into a food processor or blender with the yogurt, orange juice and honey, if using, and process until smooth.

Pour the smoothie into a glass over ice, if using, top with a swirl of any remaining yogurt and serve immediately.

For peach, pear & raspberry smoothie, blend 1 peach and 1 pear and with 125 g (4 oz) raspberries. Add 150 ml (¼ pint) peach juice to make a tangy drink.

marbled peach milkshake

Makes **900 ml (1½ pints)**

300 g (10 oz) **raspberries**
4 teaspoons **clear honey**
2 large juicy **peaches**
1 teaspoon **vanilla bean
  paste** or a few drops
  vanilla essence
125 ml (4 fl oz) **single cream**
150 ml (¼ pint) **orange juice**

Put the raspberries in a food processor or blender and process to make a smooth purée. Press this through a non-metallic strainer to remove the seeds, and stir in half the honey. Check the sweetness, adding a little more honey if necessary.

Halve the peaches, remove the stones and coarsely chop the flesh. Blend the peaches to a purée with the vanilla bean paste or essence and cream. Blend in the orange juice and any remaining honey.

Spoon a layer of the peach purée to a depth of about 15 mm (¾ inch) in 2 large glasses. Add a layer of raspberry puree and repeat the layering. Lightly marble the colours together with a knife and serve.

For vanilla yogurt smoothie, blend 175 ml (6 fl oz) plain live yogurt with 1 teaspoon vanilla bean paste, 2 tablespoons clear honey and 300 ml (½ pint) apple juice.

rhubarb & custard smoothie

Makes **400 ml (14 fl oz)**

150 g (5 oz) **canned rhubarb**
150 g (5 oz) **ready-made
  custard**
100 ml (3½ fl oz) ice-cold
  semi-skimmed milk
1 teaspoon **icing sugar**
  (optional)
ice cubes (optional)

Drain the rhubarb and discard the juice.

Put the rhubarb in a food processor with the custard, milk
and icing sugar, if using, and process until smooth.

Pour the smoothie into a large glass over ice, if using, and
serve immediately.

For choco-cherry shake, blend 100 g (3½ oz) pitted
cherries with 100 ml (3½ fl oz) soya milk and 25 g (1 oz)
melted plain chocolate. Serve with ice.

dried fruit & apple smoothie

Makes **450 ml (¾ pint)**

125 g (4 oz) **dried fruit salad**
about 400 ml (14 fl oz) **apple
  juice**
200 ml (7 fl oz) **Greek yogurt**
ice cubes (optional)

Roughly chop the dried fruit salad and place it in a large
bowl. Pour over the apple juice, cover the bowl and leave to
stand overnight.

Put the dried fruit salad and apple juice in a food processor
or blender, add the yogurt and process until smooth, adding
a little more apple juice if necessary.

Pour the smoothie into 2 glasses, add a couple of ice
cubes, if using, and serve immediately.

For apricot smoothie, process 200 g (7 oz) canned
apricots in natural juice with 150 g (5 oz) apricot yogurt
and 150 ml (¼ pint) ice-cold semi-skimmed milk.

watermelon cooler

Makes **300 ml (½ pint)**

100 g (3½ oz) **watermelon**
100 g (3½ oz) **strawberries**
100 ml (3½ fl oz) **still water**
small handful of **mint or**
  tarragon leaves, plus extra
  to serve (optional)

Skin and deseed the melon and chop the flesh into cubes.
Hull the strawberries. Freeze the melon and strawberries
until solid.

Put the frozen melon and strawberries in a food processor
or blender, add the water and the mint or tarragon and
process until smooth.

Pour the mixture into 2 short glasses, decorate with mint or
tarragon leaves, if liked, and serve immediately.

For melon & almond smoothie, process 100 g (3½ oz)
frozen galia melon flesh with 100 ml (3½ fl oz) almond milk.

red pepper & tomato smoothie

Makes **200 ml (7 fl oz)**

50 g (2 oz) **red pepper**
50 g (2 oz) **cucumber**
30 g (1¼ oz) **spring onion**
100 ml (3½ fl oz) **tomato juice**
splash of **lemon juice**
splash of **hot pepper sauce**
splash of **Worcestershire
   sauce**
salt and pepper

Core and deseed the red pepper and roughly chop the flesh. Peel the cucumber and roughly chop the flesh. Roughly chop the spring onion, reserving a few shreds for a garnish.

Pour the tomato juice into a food processor or blender, add the pepper, cucumber and spring onion and process briefly. Taste, then season to taste with lemon juice, hot pepper sauce, Worcestershire sauce and salt and pepper.

Pour the smoothie into a glass, garnish with the remaining spring onion and serve immediately.

For guacamole smoothie, add 40 g (1½ oz) spring onion, half a chopped chilli, half a ripe avocado and 100 ml (3½ fl oz) tomato juice to a food processor or blender and process until smooth. Serve with ice and some chopped coriander.

juices & smoothies for kids

mango & melon juice

Makes **about 400 ml**
  (14 fl oz)

1 ripe **mango**
½ **galia melon**
200 ml (7 fl oz) **orange juice**
ice cubes

Peel the mango, remove the stone and roughly chop the flesh. Peel and deseed the galia melon and roughly chop the flesh.

Put the mango and melon in a food processor or blender, add the orange juice and a couple of ice cubes and process until smooth.

Pour the juice into 2 short glasses and serve immediately.

For grape & melon juice, juice 150 g (5 oz) galia melon flesh with 75 g (3 oz) seedless green grapes. Dilute with 150 ml (¼ pint) water.

mango, orange & cranberry juice

Makes **200 ml (7 fl oz)**

1 **mango**
1 **orange**
125 g (4 oz) **cranberries**
100 ml (3½ fl oz) **still water**
1 teaspoon **clear honey**
ice cubes (optional)

Peel the mango and remove the stone. Peel the orange and divide the flesh into segments. Juice the cranberries with the mango and orange.

Pour the juice into a glass and stir in the water and honey. Add a couple of ice cubes, if using, and serve immediately.

For kiwifruit, orange & strawberry juice, juice 2 oranges and 1 kiwifruit with 200 g (7 oz) strawberries.

melon, carrot & ginger juice

Makes **200 ml (7 fl oz)**

250 g (8 oz) **cantaloupe
  melon**
1 **lime**
1 cm (½ inch) piece **fresh root
  ginger**
125 g (4 oz) **carrot**
ice cubes, to serve (optional)

Peel and deseed the melon and cut the flesh into cubes. Peel the lime. Peel and roughly chop the ginger. Juice the carrot with the melon, lime and ginger.

Pour the juice into a glass over ice, if using, and serve immediately.

For carrot, orange & apple juice, juice 2 carrots with 1 orange and 1 apple.

pear & pineapple juice

Makes **200 ml (7 fl oz)**

200 g (7 oz) **fresh pineapple**
  or **canned pineapple in its**
  own juices
½ **lemon**
2 **pears**
ice cubes

Peel and core the fresh pineapple and cut the flesh into pieces. If using canned pineapple, drain and discard the juice. Juice the lemon with the pineapple and pears.

Pour the juice into a glass over ice and serve immediately.

For pear & kiwifruit juice, replace both the lemon and pineapple with 3 kiwifruit. This is an excellent juice for all-round good health.

apple, pineapple & melon juice

Makes **200 ml (7 fl oz)**

½ **galia melon**
¼ **pineapple**
3 **green apples**
ice cubes (optional)

Peel and deseed the melon. Remove the skin and hard
core from the pineapple. Chop all the fruit into even-sized
pieces and juice.

Pour the juice into a glass over ice, if using, and serve
immediately.

For plum & apple juice, remove the stones from 5 ripe
plums, then juice them with 3 red apples. Serve this
delicious juice over ice.

orange, apple & pear juice

Makes **200 ml (7 fl oz)**

2 **oranges**
1 **red apple**
1 **pear**
ice cubes (optional)
1 teaspoon **clear honey**
  (optional)

Peel the oranges and divide the flesh into segments. Chop the apple and pear into even-sized pieces. Juice all the fruit.

Pour the juice into a glass over ice, if using, stir in the honey, if using, and serve immediately.

For apple & pear slush, roughly chop 2 pears and 2 apples, then process the juice in a food processor or blender with some ice.

apple, peach & strawberry lollies

Makes **300 ml (12 fl oz)**

2 **peaches**
300 ml (½ pint) **still water**
1 **red apple**
125 g (4 oz) **strawberries**

Halve the peaches, remove the stones, roughly chop the flesh and juice.

Add one-third of the water and spoon the mixture into 3–4 lolly moulds. Freeze until just set.

Roughly chop the apple and juice. Add one-third of the water and pour over the frozen peach mixture. Freeze until just set.

Hull the strawberries, then juice them. Add the remainder of the water, pour over the frozen apple mixture and freeze until set.

For orange & strawberry juice, hull 200 g (7 oz) strawberries and juice them with 2 oranges.

strawberry, redcurrant & orange juice

Makes **225 ml (7½ fl oz)**

100 g (3½ oz) **strawberries**
75 g (3 oz) **redcurrants**, plus
  extra to serve (optional)
½ **orange**
125 ml (4 fl oz) **still water**
½ teaspoon **clear honey**
  (optional)
ice cubes

Hull the strawberries. Remove the stalks from the redcurrants and peel and segment the orange. Juice the fruit, add the water and stir in the honey, if using.

Pour the juice into a glass, add some ice cubes and decorate with extra redcurrants, if liked. To make this juice into lollies, pour into lolly moulds after stirring in the honey and freeze.

For kiwifruit & orange juice, roughly chop 3 kiwifruit and juice with 2 large oranges.

melon, blackberry & kiwifruit juice

Makes **200 ml (7 fl oz)**

100 g (3½ oz) **cantaloupe
  melon**
2 **kiwifruit**
100 g (3½ oz) fresh or frozen
  blackberries, plus extra to
  serve
100 ml (3½ fl oz) **apple juice**
2–3 **ice cubes**

Cut the melon into cubes but do not remove the skin.
Cut the kiwifruit into slices. Juice the blackberries with
the melon and kiwifruit.

Transfer the juice to a food processor or blender, add the
apple juice and a couple of ice cubes and process briefly.

Pour the juice into a glass, decorate with a few blackberries
and serve immediately.

For kiwifruit, melon & grape juice, roughly chop
2 kiwifruit and juice with 375 g (12 oz) honeydew melon
flesh and 125 g (4 oz) seedless green grapes. For a
change, freeze the juice in lolly moulds.

kiwifruit, melon & passionfruit juice

Makes **300 ml (10 fl oz)**

about 300 g (10 oz)
  watermelon
2 **kiwifruit**
200 ml (7 fl oz) **passionfruit
  juice**

Peel and deseed the melon and cut the flesh into cubes. Put the melon in a freezer container and freeze for at least 2 hours or overnight.

Peel and roughly chop the kiwifruit, then put them in a food processor or blender with the melon and passionfruit juice and process until thick.

Pour the juice into a large glass and serve immediately.

For kiwifruit, melon & pineapple juice, roughly chop 2 kiwifruit and juice with 300 g (10 oz) watermelon flesh and 200 ml (7 fl oz) pineapple juice.

strawberry, carrot & beetroot juice

Makes **300 ml (10 fl oz)**

250 g (8 oz) **carrot**
125 g (4 oz) **beetroot**
1 **orange**
125 g (4 oz) **strawberries**,
 plus extra to serve (optional)
ice cubes

Juice the carrot, beetroot and orange.

Hull the strawberries. Put the carrot, beetroot and orange juice in a food processor or blender, add the strawberries and a few ice cubes and process until smooth.

Pour the juice into a large glass, decorate with a strawberry, if liked, and serve immediately.

For strawberry, melon & cucumber juice, hull 100 g (3½ oz) strawberries and juice with 75 g (3 oz) honeydew melon and the same amount of cucumber.

tomato, orange & celery juice

Makes **400 ml (14 fl oz)**

2 **oranges**
2 **celery sticks**, plus leafy
  stalks to serve
4 **tomatoes**
2 **carrots**
ice cubes

Peel the oranges. Trim the celery and cut it into 5 cm (2 inch) lengths. Juice the tomatoes and carrots with the oranges and celery.

Pour the juice into 2 tall glasses over ice, decorate with leafy celery stalk stirrers and serve immediately.

For celery & apple juice, trim and cut 3 celery sticks into 5 cm (2 inch) lengths. Juice the celery with 2 apples and 25 g (1 oz) alfalfa sprouts.

mango, apple & cucumber juice

Makes **200 ml (7 fl oz)**

200 g (7 oz) **apple**
125 g (4 oz) **cucumber**
100 g (3½ oz) **mango**
ice cubes

Peel the apple and cucumber. Peel the mango, remove the stone and roughly chop the flesh. Juice with the apples and cucumber.

Transfer the juice to a food processor or blender, add a couple of ice cubes and blend to make a fruity slush. Serve immediately.

For papaya, orange & cucumber juice, juice 125 g (4 oz) papaya flesh with the same amount of cucumber and 2 oranges.

pineapple, parsnip & carrot smoothie

Makes **300 ml (10 fl oz)**

250 g (8 oz) **pineapple**, plus
  extra to serve (optional)
100 g (3½ oz) **parsnip**
100 g (3½ oz) **carrot**
75 ml (3 fl oz) **soya milk**
ice cubes

Peel the pineapple, remove the core and cut the flesh into chunks. Juice the parsnips and carrots with the pineapple.

Transfer the juice to a food processor or blender, add the soya milk and some ice cubes and process until smooth.

Pour the mixture into 2 short glasses, decorate with pineapple wedges, if liked, and serve immediately.

For carrot, orange & banana smoothie, juice 150 g (5 oz) carrot with 100 g (3½ oz) orange, then process in a food processor or blender with 100 g (3½ oz) banana and 6 dried apricots.

raspberry & blueberry smoothie

Makes **200 ml (7 fl oz)**

250 g (8 oz) **raspberries**
200 ml (7 fl oz) **apple juice**
200 g (7 oz) **blueberries**
4 tablespoons **Greek yogurt**
100 ml (3½ fl oz) **skimmed
  milk**
1 tablespoon **clear honey**,
  or to taste
1 tablespoon **wheatgerm**
  (optional)

Purée the raspberries with half the apple juice. Purée the blueberries with the remaining apple juice.

Mix together the yogurt, milk, honey and wheatgerm, if using, and add a spoonful of the raspberry purée.

Pour the blueberry purée into a tall glass. Carefully pour over the yogurt mixture, and then pour the raspberry purée over the surface of the yogurt. Serve chilled.

For vanilla berry juice, process 150 g (5 oz) frozen mixed berries with 300 ml (½ pint) vanilla-flavoured soya milk and 1 teaspoon clear honey.

mango, apple & blackcurrant smoothie

Makes **400 ml (14 fl oz)**

3 **mangoes**
2 tablespoons **mango sorbet**
100 ml (3½ fl oz) **apple juice**
200 g (7 oz) **blackcurrants or blueberries**

Peel the mangoes, remove the stones and roughly chop the flesh. Purée the mangoes with the mango sorbet and half the apple juice. Set aside to chill.

Purée the blackcurrants with the rest of the apple juice.

Spoon the mango smoothie into 2 short glasses. Place a spoon on the surface of the mango, holding it as flat as you can, and pour on the blackcurrant purée. Drag a teaspoon or skewer down the inside of the glass, to make vertical stripes around the glass.

For blueberry, apple & honey smoothie, add 200 g (7 oz) blueberries to a food processor or blender with 100 ml (3½ fl oz) apple juice, 300 ml (½ pint) natural yogurt and 2 tablespoons clear honey. Process until blended.

strawberry, mango & orange lollies

Makes **450 ml (18 fl oz)**

125 g (4 oz) **strawberries**
1 small ripe **mango**
300 ml (½ pint) **orange juice**

Hull the strawberries, then freeze them for 2 hours or overnight.

Peel the mango, remove the stone and roughly chop the flesh. Process the mango, frozen strawberries and orange juice in a food processor or blender until thick.

Pour the mixture into lolly moulds and freeze until set.

For strawberry, orange & banana smoothie, peel 1 small ripe banana and freeze along with 75 g (3 oz) strawberries for a couple of hours. Put the fruit in a food processor or blender with 250 ml (8 fl oz) orange juice and process until smooth.

banana, mango & orange smoothie

Makes **400 ml (14 fl oz)**

1 ripe **banana**
1 ripe **mango**
200 ml (7 fl oz) **orange juice**
200 ml (7 fl oz) **semi-
skimmed milk**
3 tablespoons **fromage frais**
2–3 **ice cubes**

Peel and slice the banana. Peel the mango, remove the stone and roughly chop the flesh.

Put the banana, mango, orange juice, milk, fromage frais and a couple of ice cubes in a food processor or blender and process until smooth.

Pour the mixture into 2–3 short glasses and serve immediately.

For papaya, orange & banana smoothie, process the flesh of a papaya with a banana in a food processor or blender, then add the juice of 1 orange and 300 ml (½ pint) apple juice.

kiwifruit, mango & raspberry smoothie

Makes **400 ml (14 fl oz)**

3 **kiwifruit**
150 ml (¼ pint) **lemon- or orange-flavoured yogurt**
1 small **mango**
2 tablespoons **orange or apple juice**
150 g (5 oz) **raspberries**
1–2 teaspoons **clear honey**

Peel and roughly chop the kiwifruit, then process in a food processor or blender until smooth. Spoon the purée into 2 tall glasses, and top each with a spoonful of yogurt, spreading the yogurt to the sides of the glasses.

Peel the mango, remove the stone and roughly chop the flesh. Blend the mango to a purée with the orange or apple juice and spoon it into the glasses on top of the kiwifruit purée and yogurt. Top with another layer of yogurt.

Blend the raspberries and push them through a sieve over a bowl to extract the seeds. Check their sweetness (you might need to stir in a little honey if they're very sharp) and spoon the raspberry purée into the glasses.

For mango, apple & passionfruit smoothie, juice 3 apples. Process the juice in a food processor or blender with the flesh of a mango and 2 passionfruit.

peach & orange smoothie

Makes **400 ml (14 fl oz)**

400 g (13 oz) can **peaches** in
  natural juice
150 ml (¼ pint) **peach- or
apricot-flavoured yogurt,**
  plus extra to serve
200 ml (7 fl oz) **orange juice**
clear honey (optional)
2–3 **ice cubes** (optional)

Drain the peaches, discarding the juice, and put them in
a food processor or blender with the yogurt, orange juice,
honey, if using, and a couple of ice cubes, if liked. Process
until smooth.

Pour the mixture into 2 short glasses and top with a swirl
of any remaining yogurt.

For citrus yogurt smoothie, put 200 g (7 oz) canned
grapefruit in natural juice in a food processor or blender
with 150 ml (5 fl oz) lemon-flavoured yogurt and 150 ml
(¼ pint) semi-skimmed milk. Process until smooth.

peach smoothie

Makes **200 ml (7 fl oz)**

1 large **peach**
150 ml (¼ pint) **natural yogurt**
50 ml (2 fl oz) **milk**
raspberries, to decorate

Skin the peach, remove the stone and roughly chop the flesh. Put the peach, yogurt and milk in a food processor or blender and process until smooth.

Pour the smoothie into a glass, decorate with raspberries and serve immediately.

For pineapple, banana & strawberry smoothie, juice 100 g (3½ oz) strawberries with 300 g (10 oz) pineapple. Put the juice in a food processor or blender, add a banana and process until smooth.

strawberry & soya smoothie

Makes **200 ml (7 fl oz)**

100 g (3½ oz) fresh or frozen
  strawberries
200 ml (7 fl oz) **soya milk**
2 **kiwifruit**
ice cubes (optional)
25 g (1 oz) **flaked almonds**,
  to decorate (optional)

Hull the strawberries. Put them into a food processor or blender with the soya milk and kiwifruit and process briefly. If you are using fresh rather than frozen strawberries add a few ice cubes, if using, and process until smooth.

Pour the mixture into a glass, decorate with flaked almonds, if liked, and serve immediately

For summer berry & honey smoothie, put 125 g (4 oz) frozen mixed berries into a food processor or blender with 300 ml (½ pint) grape juice, 3 tablespoons quark and 1 teaspoon clear honey. Process until smooth.

banana & chocolate smoothie

Makes **400 ml (14 fl oz)**

1 **banana**
2 tablespoons organic **cocoa
  powder**
300 ml (½ pint) **semi-
  skimmed milk**
100 ml (3½ fl oz) **apple juice**
2 large scoops vanilla **ice
  cream**
**cocoa powder or chocolate
  shavings**, to decorate

Peel and roughly chop the banana. Place in a food
processor or blender with the cocoa powder, milk, apple
juice and ice cream and process until smooth.

Pour the mixture into 2 tall glasses, dust with cocoa
powder or chocolate shavings and serve.

For banana & peanut butter smoothie, put a banana,
300 ml (½ pint) semi-skimmed milk and a tablespoon of
smooth peanut butter into a food processor or blender
and process until smooth.

banana & mango smoothie

Makes **600 ml (1 pint)**

1 large **banana**, plus extra to
  serve (optional)
1 large ripe **mango**
150 ml (5 fl oz) **natural yogurt**
300 ml (½ pint) **pineapple
  juice**

Peel and slice the banana, then put it in a freezer container
and freeze for at least 2 hours or overnight.

Peel the mango, remove the stone and cut the flesh into
cubes.

Put the frozen banana, mango, yogurt and pineapple juice
into a food processor or blender, process until smooth.

Pour the mixture into 3 glasses, decorate with a slice of
banana, if liked, and serve immediately.

For cinnamon yogurt banana smoothie, blend a small
ripe banana with 250 ml (8 fl oz) plain live yogurt, a pinch
of cinnamon and clear honey, to taste.

index

acknowledgements

Executive Editor Nicky Hill
Contributing Editor Sarah Ford
Editor Lisa John
Executive Art Editor Mark Stevens
Designer Geoff Borin
Photographer Lis Parsons
Home Economist Alice Storey
Prop Stylist Liz Hippisley
Senior Production Controller Martin Croshaw

Commissioned photography © Octopus Publishing Group Limited/Lis Parsons apart from the following: Octopus Publishing Group Limited/Gareth Sambridge 11, 13, 24, 24, 26, 34, 86, 130, 170, 180; /Janine Hosegood 12, 28, 36, 76, 90; /Jeremy Hopley 64; /Karen Thomas 152; /Stephen Conroy 8; /Vanessa Davies 9, 186, 188, 205, 210, 214, 216, 222, 224, 230.